enchantment

Meditations on the Divine

by

Benjamin Lamberton

London

Information about sources and artworks referenced in the text may be found in the endnotes.

In memory of
Helen Lamberton Gates

Contents

Encounters and What's in This Book

I have always been intrigued by human perceptions of the divine. I was fascinated by the myriad ways in which humans sought divinity: the odd cults, the strange liturgies, the multiple gods, angels, saints, and martyrs. But I was aloof about what I studied, disdainful of these weird enthusiasms. Then, in midlife, I was clobbered by the reality of the dynamic I had been playing with.

Here's how it happened. My wife Mary and I were living in Washington, D.C. at the time. My law firm was about three miles from our house. By marvelous luck, I could walk nearly the entire way through parkland. My route took me along a path beside a creek. There were hills running on either side of the path, and the hills were thickly wooded. Sycamores grew along the stream, beech, oak, and tulip trees predominated on the hills.

It was a beautiful walk, eventually terminating at the Potomac River. From there, I walked east along the towpath that ran beside the Chesapeake and Ohio Canal.

When I came south on the path in the morning, I met other walkers, some with dogs. There were also runners, although the track had an uneven surface. But it was different at night. Then it was completely deserted. In ten years, I met only one other walker using the path at night.

I was addicted to walking the path at night. Moonlight provided enough illumination to make my way for at least a week every month – and when the sky was overcast, refracted light from the city was enough to stay on the path. It was harder on clear moonless nights. Still I could feel my way.

On those dark nights there were bright stars shining through the striped branches of winter trees. The stars seemed attached to the trees. *Tree stars* I called them – or were they *star trees*? In winter, as I felt my way up the path, I watched the sky and loved it. As I watched, the stars seemed to coalesce into figures – into faces. Not the conventional constellations, but something new.

In particular, I found myself accompanied by a star-being who seemed to watch me – a friendly presence.

In the secrecy of these woods at night, I took to dancing to this star-being. I danced exuberantly, the capering of a fool in the dark, but a joyful and delighted fool. I had the sense that my companionable star-being liked my play. Winking, the star-being seemed to come with me in my breathless cavorts as I went north towards home.

I played with the star-being for several years. I would arrive at the far end of the park feeling replete. I was opened, at liberty, and very happy.

I did not think much about what I was dancing with on my dark passages. A forest deity perhaps. Sometimes I called my star-being a pig god, because his face was broad like that of a pig. I did not realize that I was playing with divinity.

On my forty-fourth birthday something happened. My office was in Georgetown, the oldest part of Washington. I was born at six o'clock on March 8, 1940, just a few blocks away from my office, at the old Georgetown University Hospital. On my birthday, I was sitting in my office, going over some documents. A storm was brewing outside. The sky darkened. Thunder rumbled and then there were several flashes of lightning. This was very unusual in March. Then it began to snow hard – big flakes of soft wet snow. I suddenly had the feeling that this storm was a birthday present for me.

I grabbed my coat and rushed outside. The snow was tumbling down. Bangs of explosive thunder and lightning ricocheted around. I was awed. I made my way towards the old Georgetown Hospital. As I crossed the canal, an ancient tree that hung over the towpath collapsed and hit the towpath with a thud. The snow was accumulating. Traffic was at a standstill on M Street, cars sliding into the curb and each other. Panicked drivers spun their wheels. I crossed, climbed the hill and turned west on O Street, over the snow-covered cobbles. Beside the old hospital there was a raucous outburst of thunder and lightning. It was exactly six o'clock.

The snow was blinding. I slid and stumbled my way along Reservoir Road. Traffic was stationary. I crossed the road and ducked down to the path. Cold wet snow was up to my ankles. It was silent as the sounds of the traffic fell away. Through the veil of the falling snow, I saw the branches of every tree covered with white. Small trees and brambles bent under the heavy weight. The stark winter forest symmetry was transformed.

Awe penetrated my gut, deep cold wet breath chilled the depth of my being. I walked slowly, enraptured.

Halfway up the path, four sycamores grew on the far side of the stream. On their rough bark the storm had written snow runes. It was perfectly silent except for the soft sound of falling snow. I stayed, watched, and felt the gift come up into me through my cold wet feet.

I got home eventually. A fire was burning in the fireplace. Mary and the children were delighted with the snow and looking forward to a birthday dinner.

Then, I suppose I went into a state of shock. I was thoroughly frightened. I believed that the storm was indeed a birthday present from the star-being to me. But it had never before occurred to me that my star-being was something real and powerful – not just the creation of my imagination.

I am ashamed to say that I stayed out of the woods at night after that. I was too baffled to risk a repeat of my birthday magic. I was embarrassed to be neglecting my friend, but I did not go back to see him.

Worse was to come. I began to take pride in the fact that an amazing being had given me such a birthday gift. While I didn't dare to go see the star-being, I bragged about my experience to a few friends – especially young friends I wanted to impress.

My life became busier. I worked hard at the office and there were many events that filled evenings and weekends. But I felt a sadness. I had betrayed the star-being.

Ten years passed. Viewed externally, I lived an ordinary life. And after ten years, I found it hard to believe what seemed to have happened on my forty-fourth birthday.

Then one evening, I took our Labrador, Jasper, out for a walk in Battery Kemble Park, another heavily wooded park close to us. It was a clear moonless night. While Jasper dashed ahead, I felt my way down the steep path. We came into the meadow at the bottom of the hill, and then circled around the park, up the far hill, and then back down. Finally, we started up the steep path towards home, Jasper beside me.

Suddenly there was a brilliant light just above the trees – just to the left of us. A figure was in the midst of this light. The appearance was sharp and abrupt. I felt rather than heard a huge burst of sound. The ground jerked. I fell, stunned. Jasper bolted then ran in circles barking.

I lay on the ground immobilized. The light disappeared as suddenly as it appeared. I smelled the earth. I did not want to go anywhere. My mind stood still.

Jasper gradually calmed and came back. As I struggled to get to my feet, I felt a sharp pain in my ankle. I was nauseous. With the aid of a fallen branch within my reach, I finally was able to get myself upright and struggled up the hill. We somehow got home. Mary took me over to the hospital. My ankle was broken. They put a cast on me and sent us home. Later, I had a look at Jasper. The eye on his left side seemed to be cauterized. It was tightly shut, and the area around it seemed parched. Happily, he didn't seem to be in pain. I took him to the vet the next day. The vet was puzzled – I didn't tell him what I believed had caused the problem. He gave me some salve to put around the eye.

So, there I was, ten years later, terrified again. The being in the brilliant light was very angry. He did not seem to be the same as the star-being I earlier had come to know so well. This one was harsh and focused and had a directive for me that I was not at liberty to ignore.

In my mind, I called him the *sky-critter* – but that slightly derisive designation in no way denigrated the power I felt he had over me. I had to do something immediately. But just what I was supposed to do was a total puzzle to me.

I turned it over in my head. Twice I had encountered power that was beyond reality. The star-being had been playful and companionable, and there was love between us. But when I was shown that the star-being was real and valued me enough to give me an amazing birthday present, I was too shaken to continue our relationship. It meant acknowledging a breach in the rational world I had built my life around. Up until now I could play with the star-being so long as I could believe he was a whimsy, a conceit of my imagination. Once he became reality, I scarpered.

The sky-critter foreclosed the possibility of running away again. He was real. Actual. I could not dismiss him as a creature of my imagination. Now, he was the most compelling feature of my reality. And, of course, his appearance compelled me to acknowledge that the star-being was real too. My system of perception based on the attractive but mundane verities of what we call a normal life had been irrevocably broken.

But I still had to pay the mortgage and school fees. My professional practice was demanding. I had no time. I realized that unless I acted on the sky-critter's orders, my next encounter with the power was going to be even more terrifying than my encounter in Battery Kemble Park.

I am a bookish person. Professionally, I love doing research – going to the law library and piling books around me, trying to find solutions to my clients' problems in precedents, cases decided on similar facts in the past.

So I decided I would start at the library – not the law library this time, but the theological library. There was a wonderful one connected to a Methodist seminary near us. I talked to my tolerant wife, and she agreed that I could disappear on Saturdays, and do research. But research on what? Well, the Bible story I was most fascinated with was Job. I decided I would just plunge in with Job.

That began a long period of study and thinking. When I retired, I had more time and began to write. I began ambitiously. I wrote a novel that was to be my book of revelation. I was not happy with it when I finished. So, I junked the end, and wrote it again. I was still unhappy with it. Then I decided to write short pieces that would focus on particular experiences. That is what's in this book.

Pilgrims

As I started my exploration of Job, I realized that I had other source material to work with. Beginning with early childhood and continuing through life, I had had encounters with luminous beings in dreams and also in one early vision. I had held onto these encounters in my memory, but only fleetingly given credence to them as manifestations of a profound reality. Now I relived them with wonder, recognizing that they were signposts that would help me find my way.

My earliest encounter now seemed pertinent. I was four years old. My mother, sister and I were spending the summer of 1944 traveling to see grandmothers and cousins. Our final destination was my paternal grandmother's house in Maryland, a lovely Federal-style house forty miles west of Baltimore. I was put down for a nap in a cool high-ceilinged bedroom, and as I dozed, I saw through the big window in front of me an amazing sight: a line of people walking along the flat roof of the front porch. They walked along in single file. I could see them in outline only. I watched, fascinated.

I remembered this vision clearly, and its reality returned to me later in life. As a grown man, I dreamed of this line of people. They came along a beach, walking parallel to rough surf. It was night. The waves would come over them, but they held together and struggled forward. They seemed very strong and very patient, but sorely tested.

I called them the pilgrims, and now, as I embarked on my endeavor, I felt I was joining this line. Our destination was unknown, but the struggle of the journey was a reality.

Called to Silence

Frivolous attractions often lead me to what I need spiritually. I then needed silence but did not know it. The attractive blue binding of a book in a bookshop opened the door for me.

I saw this book immediately upon entering the shop. The blue of its binding was sublime. Sky blue. I walked over, and pulled the book down. *The Cloud of Unknowing*. No author identified. I had never heard of it. But the name appealed to me, along with the book's beauty, so I bought it.

It sat on my desk for a while, and then one evening I plunged in. Frankly, I could not make heads or tails of it. Luckily, there was an introduction by Laurence Freeman. I learned that the book was a manual written by a 14th century contemplative monk as a guide for a younger monk.

This sparked my own attempt at the contemplative life. I found that in the U.K. and the U.S., there were movements, initially led by Roman Catholic monks, to rediscover the ancient roots of Christian contemplative life. The tradition goes back to the 4th century Desert Fathers, and had flowered in 14th century England with the mystics Richard Rolle and Julian of Norwich together with the unknown author of the *Cloud*.

Silent prayer is at the core of this tradition. This is meditative prayer. No praise is given, no intercession asked. The *Cloud* invites us to maintain not only external silence, but internal silence as well.

I tried this and it was very hard. It was hard enough being quiet for a half an hour, but the *Cloud*'s insistence on *internal* silence was nearly impossible to achieve. Immediately, a to-do list would pop into my mind, or the sudden memory that I needed to pick up a chicken for dinner. I had a hyperactive monkey mind, as the Buddha put it. Internal silence was very difficult.

I found that the author of the *Cloud* anticipated the problem, and recommended that we choose a word that would become to us a sacred word. When the stray thought intrudes into our minds, we should invoke the word, and gently let the thought leave us. Following the advice of John Main, an English Benedictine, I use the ancient Christian prayer "Maranatha" ("come Lord") as my word.

This is not a Sunday-only activity. We are urged to enter the silence twice each day – or at least once a day. Twenty minutes in the silence, sitting upright and breathing deeply. Then an equal time simply sitting quietly.

There is an austerity to this tradition. The *Cloud* insists that in entering into silent prayer you take nothing with you. Most of us who grow up with Christianity have an internal picture of Jesus, and even an internal picture of God. We are directed by the *Cloud* to leave these behind, so that we go into the process naked. We open ourselves, and ask for nothing.

In faith, we risk meeting the actuality of Divinity, not our imagined God. We deliberately open ourselves to the Spirit, and live in hope that the Spirit will come.

And to my surprise, the Spirit came and still comes. It's not a dramatic process, but as I worked with contemplative prayer, I began to know the Spirit.

At first, there was some painfulness to this interaction. I had a well-developed ego system. I had built around me a mental abode – a house, complete with furniture and comfortable places to lounge. Each overstuffed chair was upholstered with prejudices and well-worn grievances. This was my *me*, and by middle age when I took the first steps in the contemplative life, the abode of my *me* was comfortable – even impressive. Exposing myself in prayer to the Spirit began to destroy my carefully arranged habitation. The Spirit knocked out the windows, threw out the books, chucked the furniture, and eventually knocked down the walls. Not right away, but the process moved along at a deliberate pace.

The loss of pieces of my ego structure has been painful at times. But the rewards of the endeavor are amazing. Right after a session of prayer, perception becomes luminous. I often meditate outside, and as I emerge from the silence, the natural world around me takes on a nearly magical beauty. In one group with whom I meditated, we read the Gospel immediately after emerging from the silence. In those moments when the judgmental mind was completely at rest, the Gospel had a compelling freshness – as if it were new.

There have been rich rewards to meditation in spite of the fact that my efforts to remain internally silent are usually unsuccessful. In any twenty minutes of prayer, I may achieve internal silence for only three or four minutes. The imperfection seems to make little difference. The Spirit is generous.

Contemplative prayer is an adventure that anyone can undertake. It requires no knowledge of scripture, no theological background, no analytical intelligence. What is required is patience and bravery. Definitely bravery – one does not lightly expose oneself to the actuality of Divinity even in small doses.

After engaging in contemplative prayer for a few years, I have come to feel a close relatedness with other people, even strangers. This can happen on the Underground, in crowds – anywhere. This sense of relatedness has made me far more curious about other lives, and more concerned for others. I feel as if I have a stake in their lives and they have a stake in mine. I look for sacredness in the stranger's face.

Halfway Is Enough

We human beings are not too good at uniting with the sacred. Our bodies make too many demands on us. Maybe you are sitting in meditation. Maybe your super active hormones project onto your mind's screen an attractive human. And maybe that attractive human being is doing something that pushes your sexual arousal button. You feel an urgency that distracts you just a little bit – or totally. This has been going on a very long time. Saint Antony of the Desert was a deeply committed contemplative monk, but subject to the most erotic distractions. Antony's temptations were favored by medieval artists.

It's not necessarily sex. It may be a cramp in your leg. It may be a fly that is gaily traipsing across your hand.

These body-sourced distractions are a problem because there is delight in deep meditation – delight in dwelling on the cusp of the Savior's energy, with your body at peace.

But the Risen One has been human. He/she has felt what you feel and does not judge you. In fact, we know that making it halfway is more than enough. Consider the story of Saint Martin. Martin was in his teens. Against his will he was serving as a Roman officer under the Emperor Constantine in the 4th century. One winter day Martin was passing through the gates of Amiens on his horse when he saw a beggar who was naked but for a few rags. The beggar was very cold. Martin took his sword and cut his cloak in half, and gave half his cloak to the beggar.

Now, you might think that Martin was a little stingy. Why not the whole cloak? If the beggar put the half cloak Martin gave him around his shoulders, would it cover his bum? Probably not. And surely Martin had another cloak back in his barracks. But we see that half a cloak was enough. That night Martin saw Jesus in a dream – and Jesus was wearing that half of the cloak Martin had given to the beggar. And Jesus said, "Martin gave me this cloak to cover myself." And it did.

We won't achieve perfection. There will almost always be something holding us back. Our minds in meditation will stray, often interrupted by the imperatives of our body. But the Risen One who dwells within us always comes to meet us, even if we've progressed just a little on the journey.

He will love you just as he loved Martin.

Life Giver

For many years I struggled to contain my experience of divinity within the Trinity. My soul was awake to Jesus, and watchful for the Holy Spirit in its many manifestations, but God, the first person of the Trinity, remained alien to me. I was a member of the Episcopal Church in the United States at the time.

The God of Genesis, the God who unleashed the first holocaust with his Flood, the God to whom Our Lord surrendered in obedience when he stretched out his arms upon the cross – that being I could not find in my soul. But I struggled to somehow accommodate God the Father because I was attracted to the mystery of one God in three. And I was trying to keep my spiritual life within the doctrines of the Episcopal Church.

In this struggle, I had put aside an encounter with a divine being that did not fit with my hankering for orthodoxy.

My encounter occurred fifty years ago in a dream. I was walking through the woods. I was following an emaciated, utterly exhausted man. I knew he was Jesus because he smelt like sandalwood.

He led me to a clearing. Then he pointed to a powerful glow of light on the other side of the clearing. After pointing the way, he turned and laid down in a rotting coffin.

I went in the direction he pointed. Out of the woods, the sunlight was intense. On the far side of the clearing I saw an amazing sight: a figure, perhaps half again as big as a man, sitting Buddha-like in serene meditation, his eyes half closed. He was covered with a viscous substance, perhaps semen, perhaps ghee, and all over his naked body was every form of life. Beautiful insects crawled on his skin, flowers seemed to grow out of him, and in front of him were animals of every sort, all seeking the delight of his physical being.

I have referred to the figure as *him*. But the figure transcended gender, while at the same time pulsing with a serene endlessly fecundating energy. He or she was pollinating the world.

The Me That Is Not Mine

I cannot get there without meditation. Meditation opens me. The senses are no longer directed by purpose. Perception broadens. Meditation brings awareness to these changes. My ears hear wind moving old leaves across grass. Soft cold air rests against my cheek. Through the soles of my feet I sense the dark abode of roots, of fungi, of waiting life.

There is a sudden bird call. Declarations of indignation by waterfowl. Geese pulling at the grass, moving step by step toward me. The scramble of a squirrel, the rasping traction of its feet on the rough bark of a sweet chestnut. The breath slowing, deepening, expanding space, caressing my belly, softening my throat, assuaging the hard tension in my face.

My eyes closed, the meditation deepens, interrupted by bits of conversation just heard, fragments of fantasy, a neglected grievance. These are falling away now, dissolved by the sensuality of silence, the silence moving inward, possessing the body, disassembling the mind.

Time has suspended. And so I dwell in myself, but myself, my *me*, is porous now. My *me* is the sounds I hear, the sensations I feel. The walls have fallen. I am the soft dark richness beneath my feet. I am the cold sharp air on my cheek.

I am in the fullness, at peace.

Slowly, I open my eyes. My body is peaceful in stillness, held by my steady breath. My eyes, shy at first, rest on the rough grass at my feet: tumbled, fluted, wind-made forms, worn by winter, meshed with damp leaf fragments. Wet grass and leaf fragments shine. This too is me. I close my eyes, rest in meditation, and then open them again. My eyes follow the gentle contour of the earth, here and there a fallen branch, to the massive trunk of an oak. The tree's juncture with the earth, the spreading base of the bole, holds me. I breathe and watch. The roots plunge into the earth's darkness.

Then my eyes move upward. The trunk is anciently torqued. A reddish streak on the bark climbs to where the trunk shifts leftward, birthing two great limbs, and then climbs again. My eyes move upward to the junction of eight huge arms, eight trunks, each culminating in a complex of branches. And then to the top, each limb climaxing in a furious twist of bare twigs. The crown lies flat against the slate sky.

My breath holds the meditation, and absorbs the majesty of the oak. Yes, it too is me.

I am emerging now from the meditation. And my mind asks, "How can I claim that this oak, this lofty being, is me?" From a distance my soul responds, "it can be me because this me of the deep breath, of the fullness, of the utter porousness, is not mine. It has no boundaries. It belongs to the earth, to the wind, to the oak itself, to anyone who seeks it."

Maybe

God is a problem for many of us. As conceived in the Judeo-Christian tradition, God often gets in the way of our spiritual development. The God of Genesis caused the first holocaust. God found humankind wicked, and so he destroyed virtually all life. Humans later followed God's example, and killed Jews, or Roma, or gays simply for being themselves. The God of Genesis was the enabler of subsequent holocausts.

Humans were not as thorough as God. God killed off all humanity except Noah and his dreary family. Of course, one can say, "Oh, the Flood is just a myth." But that doesn't cut it. God's adherents insist that God caused the Flood. So I am afraid we're stuck with it. If you deny God caused the first holocaust then the whole edifice crumbles.

The Flood was not the only despicable act by God. Watch what God did to Adam and Eve. He deliberately baited them to eat the fruit of the tree of good and evil, and when they did, cursed them before throwing them out of the Garden of Eden. He cursed women in particular with his mandate that they would give birth in agony. Not nice.

So how can this be explained? How can we be reconciled to God and God to us?

Maybe we misunderstand creation. Genesis tells us that the Creator was neither male nor female. That's exciting. The Creator was androgynous, as much female as male. Now watch: that means that we can refer to the Creator as *she* – she is as much a she as a he. Try calling the Creator she.

Watch as she creates through the first six days. Look how much more comfortable that is. No more creation through fiat. If the Creator is she, then she has a womb, and creation could have been made within her womb. It is no longer the Word which dictates the form of creation, but the Creator's nurturing being that creates. And if she is pregnant with creation, surely she sang. Perhaps it was her song that gave creation its form.

That still leaves the problem of this vengeful God. Well, maybe there is an explanation for that. We are told that Adam was made in the image of the Creator. So Adam started as an androgyny, neither male nor female, but both. Then we are told that the Creator pulled a rib out of the androgynous Adam, and made Eve. Male and female were now split – separated – in the human species. Did that have an impact on the Creator? Remember, humans were made in the image of the Creator. That tells us that the Creator is in the image of the human. What does that mean? I think it means that when Adam split into male and female, the Creator split too. Split into male and female.

Now something terrible happens. Adam loved Eve and Eve loved Adam. But that male remnant of the Creator did not love his now independent female remnant. The divine *he-being* was terrified of the divine *she-being* and turned his back on her.

We refer to the he remnant as "God." And the female remnant? She fled as pure energy, the energy of creation. The male being, God, could no longer create. There is another bit of fall-out from this tragedy. God feared Adam and Eve. He believed that Adam had somehow split him in two. He watches the two humans with suspicion.

Now, consider: it is this all-male being that holds center stage as "God" in the Bible. And it is this all-male being who mandates a paternalistic culture. And probably it is this all-male being who spooks you when you are told that the contemplative process will lead to you becoming one with God.

In fact, through the millennia, there was and is a complex dynamic occurring between God and humans that gradually wears down the pure maleness of God. It unwinds over centuries and centuries, and, ultimately, that dynamic leads us to Jesus of Nazareth.

As you read the Bible, you can't help but notice that God becomes less and less involved with the human world as time goes by. And perhaps this tells us that God becomes more and more lonely. Perhaps also he becomes more reflective, and perhaps more aware of his sins against humanity. So he does something utterly radical. He decides that the only way he can become reconciled with humans is for he himself to come into the world as a human, and as a human seek forgiveness for his sins against humanity. And so he does. He comes into the world as Jesus of Nazareth. Jesus is utterly defenseless. He is not even armed with the knowledge of who he is.

God leaves his judgment seat empty. With Jesus's birth there is no God in heaven. Was that absence felt on earth? Was God's presence on the judgment seat a brake on human evil? Would the slaughter of the innocents have occurred if

God had not vacated his judgment seat in order to become incarnate as Jesus of Nazareth? The answer is unknowable.

In Jesus's ministry, his divinity is gradually manifest. But it is clear that Jesus himself does not realize who he is. He asks his disciples "Who do people say I am?" And on the cross, we are told of that terrible moment when he asks God why God has forsaken him. Could it be that in the next moments, in his terrible suffering, he finally realizes that he is God – and perhaps concludes that he has utterly failed in his mission.

Then comes the great mystery – Jesus's journey into the womb of the earth. "On the second day he descended into hell." The so-called "Harrowing of Hell." What happened there? We are not told. But I think that he became whole again. I think that the terrible split of the Creator into male and female ended there. I think he was enrapt in the energy of the female and nurtured into one being who transcended sexual division. And the union of the divine male with the divine female gave rise to a huge energy – the energy of the resurrection. Embodying this wonderous nurturing energy Jesus quietly returns to the world. Because he is so transformed that at first he is not recognized even by Mary Magdalene.

Did he return to his throne of judgment to judge the quick and the dead? I don't think so. I think he took up a new abode. He came to dwell in the hearts of humans – he took up residence in every woman, every man, and every child. In our hearts he awaits us, the Creator herself, God himself.

Maybe this is what happened. But maybe not.

Brownfields

You can see them from the window of a train: old abandoned factories, and next to them moribund yards, generally paved with asphalt. These yards are so compacted nothing can grow on them. They are called "brownfields" and they are souvenirs of the industrial age. Think of their formation: years and years of heavy equipment rolling over them, compacting the soil below, leaving them lifeless.

That soil underneath – could it ever be free? Could it ever again feel the rain, feel the sunshine, feel seeds falling on it?

Your train zooms by. The brownfield is gone. But don't forget it. Because we are like that. Most of us are brownfields. Spiritual brownfields. Our souls – indeed, our minds – are encased by an impervious rind thickening over years and years by fear, anger, and boredom. Habit, tradition, the threat of disapproval, all those things have encased us in deadness. We are so compacted that we aren't open to life; we can't even see what is actually there. Oh, we function. We go to work. We cook dinner. But our consciousness is constricted. Will we ever be free? Will we ever dance to the piper at the gates of dawn?

If you have the opportunity, get off the train, and go back and look at that brownfield. Look, there is some life here. Weeds are growing in the cracks. Tough rugged weeds. They are what's called "ruderals."

Ruderals are aggressive, opportunistic. Botanical bandits. Some distance off one of its kind bloomed last summer. In the autumn, its flowers went to seed. Wind carried the seeds here and there and everywhere, and one of those seeds landed in a crack in the asphalt. Watch what it's doing. The seed has germinated, and the plant's roots are pushing down below that compacted surface, making space for itself, and expanding the crack. With enough ruderals the surface will be broken up, broken up until the long dead soil below is liberated, and again feels the rain and the sunlight.

We can see the brownfield, but our senses cannot readily perceive what divides us from a richer life. Actually, we may like being deadened. We want success, and perhaps we dimly perceive that if our souls were free, we might be hobbled in achieving ambitions. We may be dimly aware that free souls wander and play. So we talk the talk, we buzz with the lingo of our trade, we feed the egos of our seniors, and gradually that membrane separating us from the spirit becomes thicker and leatherier. But on some level, we feel the lack. We do not really like being a wasteland.

Even one ruderal can start the process of liberation. You are on the underground. You want a seat. You want to review your notes for the meeting. There is an old lady, and with her is a young child, a grandchild perhaps. The grandchild is occupying the seat next to her. Why doesn't the grandmother take the child in her lap? You get more and more annoyed. Outraged. Damn it! Then, suddenly, you just give up. "Oh, whatever!" you say to yourself. For a moment your mind is empty. You watch them. Look how easy they are together. Look how the child responds to his granny's smile, her caress. The old lady puts her head down near the child's head. She is softly singing to the child. Now the child sings the same song to his granny. They laugh. "More!" demands the child. And the old lady sings again. Suddenly she looks up and sees you.

"Oh, how inconsiderate of me! Noah can sit in my lap. Here! Here's a seat."

You sit down. You begin to pull your notes out of your bag, but you realize that Noah is staring at you. Big beautiful eyes. He ponders you. Well, he seems to approve of you. And now the child is singing to you, that same song his granny sang to him. He expects you will now sing to him – and you find yourself doing just that. Noah looks back at his granny, and she sings the song again. She glances at you. Now you and granny are allies. You both want to delight the child. You reach your stop, you say goodbye to adorable Noah and his granny, and climb up the stairs. You are so happy. You feel like a flower.

Oh! Be careful! A ruderal is taking root in you. Suddenly all the jargon, all those programmed objectives so carefully articulated, all the clever contributions you intended to make at the meeting, all seem empty. You're hungry for that feeling Noah and his granny gave you. You don't go to lunch with the others. You get a sandwich and go to the park. It's a beautiful day. You lie back on the grass – and there above you, clouds. Beautiful clouds. They're playing! Like Noah. Their edges pivot around, tails of vapor traveling on the wind. Joining and separating. You sigh, sit up, and eat your sandwich. You walk back across the park. The whole place seems charged with a new energy. You feel like dancing.

You get through the rest of the day, and that night you dream. Noah crawls into your lap. He stands up. His face is right next to yours. He whispers to you: "Wake up!"

Numbed

Perhaps at the time of the Chauvet cave paintings in southern France, humans had an acuteness of consciousness that is lost today. The astonishing vitality of the paintings suggest that perhaps thirty-five thousand years ago human consciousness embraced the entirety of nature as it existed in their environment. Humans could feel in themselves the hyper-alertness of the lion hunting or the gazelle picking up the scent of a predator.

In the last two decades, botanists have learned how trees communicate – how they signal each other through their roots and through mycorrhizal fungi. Trees, and indeed plants generally, have an acute awareness of their environment, and communicate their awareness to other organisms. Perhaps early humans shared in the sentience of the oak.

Today, the world of what we call nature is largely closed to humans. We are at best observers. Yet, in a Buddhist monastery in China, the monks ordained a thousand-year-old gingko tree. If they honored the tree with ordination, it must have been because the monks could feel what the gingko feels.

Perhaps poets have caught a glimpse of this possibility. Gary Snyder writes:

> This living flowing land
> is all there is, forever

We *are* it
It sings through us–

Rainer Maria Rilke tells us to:

See everything
And ourselves in everything
Healed and whole
Forever.

When it is said that we humans are created in the image of God, that must refer to God's consciousness, and to our consciousness. The Creator's consciousness extends to the entirety of his or her creation – and the Creator's gift to us is a consciousness potentially just as deep and rich.

We suffer from a form of neuropathy. What was once a perfect unity in the cosmos of consciousness has been eroded, fragmented, and abandoned. Antony of the Desert, writing in the 4th century, tells us:

The devils and their disciples sow in our hearts every day ... their hardness of heart

And their numbness.

Numbness is what we are left with. Just like someone with neuropathy who used to be able to feel his feet, but now cannot. In our souls we are numb to the sensations of a blue heron as it launches itself into flight. Perhaps this is the meaning of the fall. By eating the fruit of the tree of good and evil the world to us became divided. We were aware of ourselves as humans, but our capacity to participate in nature's consciousness disappeared. From then on, we were observers of nature from the outside. We were no longer nature ourselves.

Douglas E. Christie says what was lost was:

> a way of seeing oneself and the world as whole and undivided.

Simultaneously with the *othering* of nature was the *othering* of the Creator. Rather than perceiving ourselves as being one with the Risen One, we see God as an agency outside of ourselves, who manages, or mismanages, the world.

Can we regain the unity with the divine? 19th century European explorers dared to go physically into the *other* by exploring the vast globe: the Amazon, the Congo basin, and Antarctica. The 21st century explorer must venture into her inner galaxy, must explore his own tender pathway to unity of consciousness with animals and plants, and must explore her own pathway to the Divine.

Trees Are Icons

I have been pondering the possibility that trees may be icons.

I have been watching trees for a long time. I especially watch mature oaks. I am fascinated at how eccentric each oak is. I watch the epicormic curve of the limbs, the sudden nexus of branch and twig creating a perfect habitat for bird and insect life. It is a nexus like a human community that births new music, new poetry, and new life.

I love watching the same oak on a sunny day, and then on a stormy day. I love watching the tree in the moonlight. The best is lying under the tree on a starry night and watching how the twigs seemed to hold the stars, as if the twigs treasured each star.

What I am seeing is creation-energy made material. An energy both ancient and contemporary – the dynamic perpetually arising out of the Divine Being. The utter uniqueness of each tree tells us that when divine energy becomes material, it reflects the manifold nature of the Creator. Just like the infinite variety among humans – each one is made in the image of the Creator, and each one is utterly different.

If each tree tells us a unique story about the Creator, we may gradually be able to understand the nature of the Creator by watching trees.

So, are trees icons? I thought about icons in the Orthodox Church, typically depictions of Jesus, the Virgin, and the saints. In the Orthodox tradition, each icon is a portal to the sacred. The icon is not simply a picture of the saint, it *is* the saint.

Is it possible that a tree could be a passageway to a spiritual reality quite beyond the confines of our practical world?

I wondered about this, and was not at all sure that trees could play this role. I decided I needed a consultation with some trees. So I went to London's Kew Gardens, entered through Lion Gate, and found a bench. The bench backed onto a holly tree behind the Japanese Garden. I meditated there.

As my meditation deepened, I had an odd sensation. A spacious energy was entering me. Can I describe it? It was a deep energy. Envision an orchestra made up solely of cellos, basses, and bassoons. Put aside the sound that orchestra would make, and instead focus solely on the vibration it would create. That low dark deep vibration would be pretty close to what I felt. This dark energy guided my meditation.

When I emerged from my meditation, I saw that trees formed an arc in front of me. About forty-five meters away was a yew. The yew was like the dark mouth of a cave leading deep into the earth. It was the pivot point of the arc. Just to my right was a shellback hickory. Further to the right were several holm oaks, the evergreen oaks of the Mediterranean. To my left, another holm oak, two Scots pines, and beyond a trio of hawthorns, their bark nearly white. Finally, an Atlas cedar.

Each tree had its own energy. The holm oaks were lyrical and generous. Their curved black limbs stretched out companionably to the other holm oaks. The hickory was tall, straight and proud. The Scots pines seemed to revel in the patches of sunlight on their bark.

The hawthorns were quite different. They were the show-stealers. Their limbs formed a dense complex torch that seemed alight. They were playful. And the youngest one impertinently proclaimed itself an icon.

The energy of the trees took possession of me, and emphatically proclaimed that yes, they were icons, each one an icon, and in combination they had the wonder of a 14th century iconostasis.

I had an answer to the riddle, and I was frankly astonished by it. I had not expected it to be so unequivocal. But then I thought back to my earlier encounters with trees. I have often been brought to a standstill by the sight of a particular tree. English oaks with tiers of huge limbs ending in bold curves. American red oaks with deeply fluted trunks. Most amazing are the ancient sweet chestnuts with huge irregularities, grotesque carbuncles jutting out from their thick boles. Ugly and fascinating. If one of these sweet chestnuts is an icon, then the sacred is inclusive of jagged, craggy, and precipitous energy.

As I thought about my earlier encounters with trees, I realized that not all trees are icons in and of themselves. For some, especially younger trees, their divinity becomes manifest only in combination with other elements. I once watched a swamp cypress growing beside a lake. The cypress began to shimmer when small waves on the lake caught the sunlight and sent reflections dancing up its trunks. The combination of elements made what I saw sacred.

When I was staring at the array of trees which initially convinced me that trees could be icons, a breeze was blowing, and this resulted in eddies of movement in the upper limbs of the trees and exciting swishing sounds. The breeze was playing the trees like musical instruments. The breeze and the treetops together, all in an instant, were creating magic.

Perhaps there is another piece of the puzzle. Trees cannot be icons unless the beholder lets them be icons. If you habitually pay no attention to trees, then a tree cannot open a passage for you. You need to pay attention and be open to possibilities.

If you do, aren't the results unnerving? If you travel through a wood, and the trees all around you hold the potentiality of being portals into the divine world, how do you keep your balance? Can a human being keep his or her sanity with so much potentiality?

It helps to define what is at stake. Trees are not going to open you to a dazzling heavenly court with choruses of angels. No, the passage promised by the tree icon is a passage to divine love. Divine love is simple, gentle, sometimes playful, always deeply enriching. Stop and stare, sit in expectant meditation, listen. It's all there for you. Trees will take you there.

Resist Power, Be Energy

What dynamic best facilitates the realization of the Divine in the world? It seems to me that there are two dynamics available to us as human beings: energy on the one hand, and power on the other. I think there is a difference between the two. Power is focused. It is tightly directed, narrowly purposeful. It arises out of human will. Often, it is birthed by anger.

In contrast, energy arises naturally. Its source is the world itself. It is here, there, everywhere. It is fluid, generous and playful. It nurtures.

The Western world is addicted to power. We value the powerful. Powerful cars, powerful weapons, powerful men. We are impressed by power. We aspire to possess it. With power we can take more, be bigger, make history. Our power addiction permeates our religion – we yearn for a powerful God. The *power and the glory*. The two go together.

But what of the other dynamic? Energy is often invisible. If it is visible, we take it for granted. As humans, we absorb energy. We can also give rise to energy. Jesus with his hands, his eyes, and his speech created a new energy. He gave it freely. That energy was his love. It is still with us. We can either magnify it or block it.

Jesus was killed by power. By individuals who had authority and power they had accumulated either by their position in society, or by ruthlessness. They used power to persecute Jesus, have him whipped and nailed to a cross.

They did this to ensure that their power would not be taken away from them.

I wonder how power became central to our culture. The answer may lie in the cultural glorification of power, particularly as the definitive male attribute. Energy, to the extent it was recognized at all, was a feminine phenomenon, barely capable of apprehension by the power-hungry male.

Cultural glorification of power reached its apogee in Michelangelo's 16th-century sculpture of David. Look at David's body. It is a perfect body. Perfect fitness. Watch the strength in the torso. Look at the power in his arms, the huge size of his hands, the big genitals.

Now shift your attention to David's face. It is tightly focused. Sharp eyes watch the enemy for the perfect opportunity to hurl the stone from his sling. This is a depiction of power.

Michelangelo's David became the male archetype in the Western world, and for four centuries has trapped us in an aggressive trigger-happy culture. Having an enemy is essential to this culture. Note too how irrelevant the natural world is to this culture – plants, trees or the earth itself plays no part except to the extent they provide material to make weapons and feed armies.

Finding an equally compelling depiction of energy is harder. But I believe a sculpture in the Victoria and Albert Museum gives us what we're looking for. It is a Chinese sculpture of the Bodhisattva Guanyin carved in the 12th century. (This sculpture may be viewed on the Victoria and Albert Museum's website. It is object number A.7-1935.)

Guanyin is one of the most popular bodhisattvas among Buddhists. For Buddhists, a bodhisattva is a human who through long meditation has reached the final stage of enlightenment and can elect to free himself of any involvement or concern with human affairs. But rather than doing so, the bodhisattva pauses, looks back at humanity in pity, and thereafter seeks to relieve human suffering.

Contrast the posture of Bodhisattva Guanyin with David. Guanyin is relaxed, tranquil. His face tells us that he is in deep meditation, his eyes only slightly open. But there is a paradox here. As you watch the folds of his garments, you sense a dynamic flow of energy – and that impression is strengthened by the rugged forms of the clouds supporting Guanyin. In spite of his stillness and tranquility, Guanyin is birthing energy. Watch how his arm reaches out. His hand is giving, and what he gives is energy.

In a Christian context, we see the depiction of energy in Andrei Rublev's 15th century Russian icon depicting the Old Testament Trinity. (You can view it on the Tretyakov Gallery's website.) This is perhaps the most famous of all icons. It shows the three angels that appeared to Abraham and Sarah when Abraham was sitting in the opening of his tent underneath the terebinth oak tree of Mamre, as described in Chapter 18 of Genesis. The three angels, deemed to be the persons of the Trinity, are united in perfect tranquility. Stillness pervades the picture. But again, that stillness gives rise to energy. And here we can see how the cruel impact of power is transformed into positive energy.

Just above the head of the central figure, usually deemed to be Jesus, is a depiction of the oak of Mamre. Note its form. It looks like a person nailed to a cross twisting in agony. It seems extraordinary that Jesus, sitting right below, is so totally tranquil. But watch what is happening. The agony of the crucified seems to pass into Jesus, and then pass through his hand as he blesses the chalice below. The energy does not stop there. It passes right down to the stream of water rushing below the angels' feet.

Can we experience these two dynamics in daily life? There is no problem seeing power, look at any newspaper. See the heroic leader threatening his enemies. Watch the missiles fly. Read about poor people harassed; outsiders and immigrants being demonized. Power, and the results of its misuse are everywhere.

Perhaps we can't see the energy but we can feel it. It is love. Jesus is the energy of love. He opens each person to the play of his energy. And he showed us how to resist and overcome power. He showed us that we ourselves, in our lives, can birth new energy. We can be energy. We can be Jesus.

Soft Eyes

I was looking at Rembrandt's *Portrait of the Artist as a Young Man* in the Walker Art Gallery in Liverpool. He presents himself in the portrait with soft eyes. I wondered. What can we tell about a person who has soft eyes?

It put me in mind of what the crew coach at an American university once told me. I said to him that he must have far too many candidates for his top boat. I asked how he selected the eight young men who would row for the university. The coach said something odd: "I only choose boys with soft eyes."

That seemed bizarre. I asked him why, and he said that the boys with soft eyes would merge into the seamless team he needed. Young men with crafty or darting eyes would "grandstand" and try to make themselves the hero of the boat, thus upsetting the dynamic he was after.

When I encounter people with soft eyes, I tend to look into their eyes – I tend, at least for a moment, to rest in their eyes. Soft eyes are deep. Resting in the softness of Jesus's eyes must have opened a person, opened them into that deep realm of love that Jesus was and is.

When Jesus selected his disciples, did he look for individuals with soft eyes? When he recruited Judas Iscariot, did Judas have soft eyes? I think of Jesus as the good shepherd. The good shepherd reaches out and rescues the lamb that has become tangled in thorns. He strokes the lamb, he holds it against his body and calms its panic. His eyes are soft.

What does it mean to have soft eyes? Perhaps it signals that the person has not built walls around themselves. We tend, as we deal with life, to insulate ourselves from the world with defense mechanisms. We insulate ourselves with preconceptions, with prejudices, with habits of how we deal with particular people or types of people. Our eyes show our wariness. But some people are able to take the risks of interacting with the world without these filters. Their boundaries are open. They are porous. Their eyes are soft. They have adventures.

Watch how Jesus worked. Through his eyes, through his hands and through his body he would draw you into himself. He was merging you with him. His words would often open the way – you were so taken aback by what he said that at least for the moment your defenses crumbled. And then he reaches out and brings you into himself, and himself into you. When that happens you feel Jesus's deep peace, the peace that passes all understanding.

Theology, words, and doctrines are dangerous. Twisting on the hook of the Creed blinds you to Jesus's everlasting inviting eyes, his everlasting inviting hands and body.

On the Tube

I keep encountering people on the London Underground, or tube, who seem to have such a congenial chemistry that we become friends then and there, for a friendship that lasts maybe seven minutes, and is consummated in a smile or maybe three lines of dialogue. It always leaves me wondering, curious about their lives, and about what a seven-minute friendship means.

Yes, seven-minute friendships. Actually, there is something more to it. I have a strong feeling that I'll encounter Jesus on the tube, so it is worth paying attention. The many people I encounter – wasn't Jesus just like them before his ministry began? These people I see, will they too one day embark on a ministry that will change the world? Is that the pregnant possibility inherent in all humans? If after his resurrection, the Lord came into each of us, took up residence in our souls, then isn't it likely that we too will at some point embark on ministry? Maybe very modestly, but maybe not modestly!

Meditation on Saxifrage

Sometime ago, my wife and I went to the Dolomites in Italy to look at alpine plants. High on the Cansiglio plateau, the botanist Massimiliano Calligola introduced us to the saxifrage.

It is a small exquisite plant. The plants we saw seemed to be growing right out of the rock, although on closer examination, I could see that it was in fact growing in tiny fissures in the rock.

Max told us that these plants literally split rocks. Thus the name – translating the Latin gives you "stone-breaker."

Apparently, the saxifrage is not content with splitting the rock with their tough roots – some also "digest" the rock. Thus, the leaves of *Saxifrage crustata* are edged in a limestone crust – if you feel it you encounter a tough serrated abrasive. Still more amazing are the small delicate flowers of the *Saxifrage crustata*: the petals themselves have calcified edges.

A puzzle this. Rock is so obdurate, such an irrefutable fact that it seems uncanny that a small flower could challenge it.

In our political and cultural life, we encounter huge monoliths. The dictatorships of the 20th and 21st centuries represent mountains of rock – rock that hold societies in tight unvarying structures, weighing heavily on the human spirit. Similarly, religious orthodoxies often hold the human spirit in a dead rock-like state.

Yet, perhaps like saxifrage, humans have the capacity to split and crumble these monoliths.

Vasily Grossman in his novel *Life and Fate* recounts an act of kindness by an ordinary soldier giving bread to a starving peasant woman in the Soviet Union during World War II. Grossman observes that an act of kindness is deeply subversive to a totalitarian system. Benefits, indeed necessities, must be exclusively controlled by the totalitarian state. Individuals are coerced by the state's power to be cruel, and withhold necessities to the needy. Acts of kindness, individuals reaching out to other individuals, breaks up the monolith of state control.

An act of kindness is a tiny flower with powerful roots – and like a saxifrage, acts of kindness can break up monoliths.

Should She Be Stoned?

In London's Dulwich Picture Gallery there is a 17th century painting titled *The Woman Taken in Adultery* by Guercino. It depicts a moment when Jesus met the rigid forces of tradition that still govern parts of the world today. (The picture may be viewed on the Dulwich Picture Gallery's website.)

Guercino's depiction of Jesus is arresting. Jesus is confronted by an elderly man, a member of the strict sect of Pharisees. We see the elderly man in profile only – a distinguished, decent-looking man.

The Pharisee is governed by the same literal regard for religious tradition as today's Iranian mullahs. He says to Jesus, "Teacher, this woman has been caught in the very act of committing adultery. Now in the law, Moses commands us to stone women of this kind. What have you got to say?"

In Guercino's picture, the woman is being held by a guard. Her face is cast down and expressionless.

Jesus's head leans slightly to the right, towards the woman. His left-hand points at her, but he does not look at her. He is looking right into the face of the Pharisee. Jesus knows that he is being set up by the Pharisee, but his eyes express no hostility. He looks into the Pharisee's face intently, his gaze both soft and alert simultaneously.

This is the Pharisee's first encounter with Jesus. Jesus's eyes draw him in. The Pharisee finds himself being softly examined and deeply understood. The old man feels the pull of the Kingdom.

Jesus bends down and starts to write in the dust with his finger. The Pharisee falls back to the circle that surrounds the woman. Unconsciously, his hand closes on the stone he carries in his robes. He watches Jesus tracing words in the dust.

Nothing happens. The crowd stands in silence. Jesus is peaceful, breathing slowly.

The woman is trying not to show her terror, but she is trembling now, and near nauseous. She once saw a woman stoned. In her mind, she hears the horrible crack of the stone hitting the woman's head. She tries to control herself and watch Jesus. What is this strange man doing?

Now, aggressive self-righteous voices, the voice of men angered and indignant, demand to know if Jesus will uphold the law. She sees stones in their hands. Jesus stands. The men fall silent.

"Let the one among you who is guiltless be the first to throw a stone at her."

There is no emotion in the voice. The men stand still, baffled. Jesus bends over, again writing in the sand. He pays no attention to the men.

She watches. Faces slowly turn towards the old Pharisee who had confronted Jesus. His face is a mask. Then he sighs, looks at Jesus, and drops the stone. He turns and walks away. Others drop their stones and follow him. The men are gone. The crowd follows.

Jesus straightens up. He looks at the woman. She looks back. She can't take it in. They have all left.

"Woman, where are they? Has no one condemned you?"

"No one, sir."

"Neither do I condemn you. Go now, and sin no more."

Words. Words of death embodied in the law, and the Word in flesh alive. Jesus mesmerizes the Pharisees by leaning down and doing what they do - writing. But he writes their words, the words of the law, in dust. The dust will be blown by the wind and trampled by many feet.

The imperative is life, and life lived abundantly. He is opening the door for the woman to live life abundantly. And he's doing something else: he is opening the door to the Kingdom for the old man.

He planted a seed in the mind of the old man when the old man confronted him. By looking into the eyes of the old Pharisee with interest and love, Jesus transformed the situation. He set about saving the life of the woman by saving the soul of the Pharisee.

It worked. When Jesus leaned down a second time, he heard the stone drop. Looking up, he saw the Pharisee's face. The woman was saved.

He talks to the woman. In that moment, she is born again into life. In spite of her actions, she is invited to go into the community, condemned by neither the Pharisees nor her savior. She is simply told to "sin no more."

What did that mean? It surely did not mean that she should never violate one of the myriad prohibitions of the law of Moses. And I don't think Jesus was commanding her never again to have sex out of wedlock. Jesus was not just giving her a second chance – it is inconceivable that Jesus would have condoned her stoning if she were again caught in adultery. No, I believe that Jesus was enjoining the woman from violating her own heart. To live life abundantly, one must live a life steeped in heart generosity. A life in which love is the wellspring of action. Jesus tells the woman to go into the community and live a life of love.

Confounded by Beauty

Vladimir Nabokov was fascinated by moths and butterflies. He studied them closely all his life. In his autobiography, *Speak, Memory*, he notes his fascination with mimicry in nature. Butterflies and moths often disguise themselves from predators by taking on the appearance of something the predators do not want to eat. Thus, the wings of a butterfly might have the appearance of a leaf. In a Darwinian context, we would assume that the leaf design in the butterfly's wings was the result of natural selection: over millions of years butterflies that had a leaf design on their wings survived predators whereas those that did not got eaten.

But Nabokov points to an amazing phenomenon. The protective mimicry in its "subtlety, exuberance, and luxury" far exceeds the predator's powers of perception.

He writes, "When a butterfly has to look like a leaf, not only are all the details of the leaf beautifully rendered but markings mimicking grub-bored holes are generously thrown in."

When a moth mimics a wasp to scare off a predator it not only resembles a wasp in shape and color, it also walks and moves its antennae in a waspish, unmothlike manner. Darwin's "struggle for life" doctrine simply cannot explain this level of mimicry.

Nabokov sees extraordinary beauty in this over-the-top mimicry. "I discovered in nature the nonutilitarian delights that I sought in art. Both were a form of magic, both were a game of intricate enchantment and deception."

What is the energy that creates this seemingly gratuitous beauty? A playful, loving energy. I think our concept of the Holy Spirit should be stretched to include this energy, and we should acknowledge that even today the Holy Spirit creates beauty all around us, beauty that has no usefulness except to cause delight.

Purbeck Meditation

Leaning against a stone wall on a dark cold day, I fall into meditation. The wind blows hard, blowing the brooding words out of my mind. When I emerge from the silence, I turn, and rest my arms on the top of the wall. I watch the newly planted wheat merge into the gentle geometry of the hilltop. Just watch as the wind blows.

I think of the moment during the Last Supper when Jesus takes bread and breaks it, and says, "this is my body." That moment when he asks them to take the bread and eat it: "eat my body in remembrance of me." And the wine: "drink my blood in remembrance of me. Eat my body and drink my blood so you will not forget me."

Maybe the body remembers better than the mind.

No ceremony here. No incense, no bells. He gently urges us to eat and drink his physical being. That urging comes again each time we have bread in our hand, or hold a glass of wine.

The Purbeck wheat is so young I can still see the rows. The stones of the wall, marked with lichens, anchor the bottom of my vision. I watch the small hardy plants that will grow high, sweep in waves to the wind, and bear heads of grain. Wheat that will be bread that can be eaten in remembrance, or just can be eaten without knowing that he made his body bread.

Perhaps he'd done it before. Perhaps he fed the five thousand with his body, taking those few loaves and joining them with his physical being so that no one went hungry.

The gift is his pulsing warm breathing body. The body that will be fixed to the cross. He does not wait. He wants us to have and to be his physical humanity before he turns into God.

Bodies. My body, an aging body that aches here and there, is cold right now. If, in meditation, we listen to our bodies, we feel him. Then he is us, so that what we see, we see with his eyes, and what we feel, we feel with his hands.

We are his body that walked on earth two thousand years ago. And he is our body that breathes and walks today.

The Silent Music of Psalm 19

Watch clouds. At night, watch the stars. Lie on the ground and look up. As you watch, listen. You may hear the silent music of the Creator.

Psalm 19 tells us why we must watch:

> The heavens declare the glory of God,
> The vault of heaven proclaims his handiwork.

Above us, day and night, the sky scripts out the reality of the Creator – her glory and her work. This truth has been told from the beginning of time, and passed on day by day and night by night.

> Day to the next day speaks,
> Night to the night hands on knowledge.

John's Gospel tells us about a beginning emerging from the Word. "In the beginning was the Word, and the Word was with God, and the Word was God." When we watch the sky, we watch what was and still is before John's beginning – we watch what was and is before the Word. The Psalm tells us this:

> No utterance at all, no speech,
> not a sound to be heard,
> but from the entire earth the design stands out,

the message reaches the whole world.

The design in the sky, the clouds shaped by wind, colored by light, the clouds ever changing, ever playful, is the "message that reaches the whole world." If you watch a cloud's edge – pivoting, joining, reaching back, laughing, a confection against the blue sky – there, in that movement, you see the proclamation of the Creator's handiwork.

On a good day, I watch the cumulus clouds floating above me being blown eastward. Their dancing borders hold my attention until I notice that above them is another layer of clouds, wisps sweeping in long thin lines moving westward. The Psalm's message is contrapuntal; a fugue spread across the heavens.

The Psalm's language that I quote above is from the *Jerusalem Bible*. The *New English Bible* translation tells us of the silent music:

> One day speaks to another,
> night with night shares its knowledge,
> and this without speech or language
> or sound of any voice.
> Their music goes out through all the earth,
> Their words reach to the end of the world.

This rich complex but silent music impresses the design and message on every natural being and thing in the world.

In the spring, holm oaks drop the leaves of the previous year as new leaves come on. The leaves fall on their faces, so that most of what we see as we walk over them are their bland backs. Lean down and flip the leaf over and you will see the design and message of the Psalm imprinted on the reverse side: an infinite variety of forms in gold, green and brown, all singing the silent music of the Creator. The message and design of the sky has fallen through summer, fall and winter on the sky-facing leaves. The design of each leaf is unique but each contains the entire message.

All that lives below the sky bears the design and message of the Creator. Watch the whorl of a boy's hair, the wrinkles of an old face, the bark of an oak or the shape of an orchid – each contains the complete message and design. Watch and listen for the silent music that even now is making the new Creation.

Job Revisited

Job is the richest man in Uz. He has many slaves, five hundred donkeys, five hundred yoke of oxen, three thousand camels, and seven thousand sheep. In addition, he has seven sons and three daughters. When he walks to the square of the city, he takes the seat of honor. When he comes, young men hold their breath, old men rise to their feet, rich men stop speaking, and men of authority shudder.

We are told that Job is a man of perfect integrity, who fears God and avoids evil. Job himself tells us what that means: "I am sinless, I have kept all his commandments, and have never strayed from his path." But Job is not so sure that his children are sinless. "Perhaps my children have sinned, and cursed God in their hearts."

These rich kids, Job's children, enjoy themselves. Every year, each of Job's sons in turn holds a banquet, and invites his brothers and sisters to his house. They party for a week. This gives Job the heebie-jeebies. He insists that after their week of carousing, all his children come to him. Then he "purifies them." This has gone on year after year.

Job enjoys the buzz created by people's fear and admiration. But for his occasional uneasiness about his children, Job lives in a pleasant trance. He enjoys the respect. And he especially enjoys the fear. Here is the world shaping itself around him – the richest and most powerful man in Uz.

Job has become a narcissist. Perhaps he was always a narcissist. People's fear and admiration feeds his narcissism.

The Biblical story is all about Job's narcissism, and his liberation from that narcissism.

In his mind, Job creates a God just like himself. That God is a narcissistic projection. But Job is not satisfied with a God that is just a projection of himself. He needs glitz, a bit of the glamor of the real thing. Job borrows a distant glimmer of true divinity. But only a glimmer – the rest of this projected God is, in fact, Job. Job sitting on his seat of honor in the marketplace with the young men holding their breath.

Job periodically calls in his managers to be sure his seven thousand sheep are increasing in numbers and his three thousand camels are being used to maximize profit. Even his wealth management meetings are mirrored in the court of his projected God. Job's God calls meetings where each of his angels report.

Just as Job creates fear – men of authority shudder in front of him – so his projection creates fear. Ironically, Job himself is scarred by his own projection. This God that he has created can do to him all the things he can do, or does do, to others.

Job senses something is wrong. He has nightmares. He does not have the insight to see that what is wrong is in himself. Instead he focuses on his children. They are the sinners.

When Job borrowed just enough of the bright energy of true divinity to make his narcissistic projection glow, he left the awesome whole of the Creator's energies both unacknowledged and unworshipped. The result is inevitable.

"Don't poach a little piece of me to decorate your false God and then deny the rest of my reality." The Creator is angry.

So here is Job's projection sitting on the seat of honor holding court in heaven. Angels are coming to report. Of course, the angels are nervous. Some hold their breath, all stand, some with less favorable reports tremble. That's exactly like what happens when Job's managers on earth come to report to Job. But on this occasion, something different happens in the heavenly assembly. A blast of energy bursts in. It is the Accusing Angel. The Accusing Angel in most translations is called "Satan." The Accusing Angel is the energy of creation – the energy that dwells in the universe, playing with the constellations. That same energy dwells somewhere in Job's long-suppressed soul.

Job's puny God is nonplussed. "Where have you come from?" He asks incredulously. And the Accusing Angel gives his enigmatic answer: "From walking here and there on earth, and looking around." Plainly, Job's wealth management meetings had never before been interrupted by anyone like this.

Proof of the puny God's identity is revealed by what happens next. Job's God says to the Accusing Angel, "Did you notice my servant, Job?" Of course he brings up Job. After all, he is Job. And the puny God brags about Job: "There is no one on earth like him: a man of perfect integrity, who fears God and avoids evil." The Accusing Angel challenges Job's puny God: Job is the exemplary human being only because the puny God has hedged protections around him, his family, and all that he owns. "But just reach out and strike everything he has, and I bet he'll curse you to your face."

Job's puny God agrees to the Accusing Angel's proposal, but with a condition: "Just don't lay a hand on him."

Why did Job's projection agree? Wasn't this Job's own God, his own creation? Why did he consent to the wholesale destruction of all Job possessions? I think the projection had become autonomous. Perhaps when narcissism becomes acute, the self-image created by the narcissist begins to have a life of its own. In its megalomania, the image attacks the poor human who projected it.

Another question: Why did the Accusing Angel want to destroy Job's property? I think because Job's wealth was his prison. Job's wealth magnified his narcissism and enabled Job's megalomania. Job's soul could not be free until his wealth was gone.

The Accusing Angel gets to work. In no time all the sheep and camels and oxen have gone. In no time all his children's houses are destroyed – and in no time his children themselves are killed. All of the things that made Job first among Uzeans are gone. Now he is jeered by the street boys. They stand beside Job and sneer. His narcissism is being destroyed.

Now we see Job's heroic stubbornness. He refuses to renounce his projected God.

So the Accusing Angel goes back to that puny God in his heaven and seeks permission to strike Job's flesh and bones. Again, the puny God gives him permission, but peevishly complains that the Accusing Angel made him torment Job for no reason. "So what?" asks the Accusing Angel. The Accusing Angel now covers Job with boils from his scalp to the soles of his feet. Job is in agony, but still refuses to curse his puny projection. Perhaps he's holding onto that glimmer of true divinity he'd incorporated in his projection.

But Job curses the day he was born. "God damn the day I was born and the night that forced me from the womb; let black clouds overwhelm it; let the sun be plucked from its sky." Then he tells us that his "worst fears have happened; my nightmares have come to life."

In his misery, Job is joined by three friends – the comforters. Eliphaz the Temanite, Bildad the Shuhite, and Zophar the Naamathite. They are neither friends nor comforters. They take a sadistic delight in Job's fall – a true example of schadenfreude: "now it is *your* turn, you tremble, now *you* are the victim, you shudder."

They insist that God would only smite Job so dreadfully if Job had sinned. Job in his misery refuses to acknowledge sin: "Can't I tell right from wrong? If I sinned, wouldn't I know it?"

Job is becoming angry. Angry at God – actually, angry at the God he made in his own image. "God has tricked me, and lured me into a trap." Job is determined to resist. "I will take my complaint to God," he says. "I want to speak before God, to present my case in God's court." He becomes more and more irate. "Can't he [God] tell right from wrong, or keep his accounts in order?" But Job hasn't been humbled. If he appears in God's court "I would justify the least of my actions; I would stand before him like a prince."

But something else is happening to Job: terrifying dreams. Plate 11 of William Blake's *Illustrations of the Book of Job* depicts one of these dreams. Job is lying prone. Lying on top of him is his mirror image, a being who looks exactly like him. It's his projection, the puny God. A serpent has its head near Job's head – scale-covered devils reach up and grab Job's body. The mirror image lying above him, holding him down, does not have feet – the mirror image has cloven hooves.

So Job is able to actually see the false God he has created.

Does Job take it in? Not fully. But we see a change in his responses to the comforters. He is beginning to seek a God beyond his puny projection. He is reaching for a savior. He yearns for "a witness in heaven, a spokesman above the clouds" who would judge between mortal and God. Perhaps conceptualizing a witness in heaven opens Job to the energy of his own soul. That opening, however small, is enough for the Whirlwind.

It is the Unnamable who speaks to Job out of the Whirlwind. "Who is this whose ignorant words smear my design with darkness?" Huge energy, perhaps no recorded verbal communication has ever packed a more terrifying punch. The Whirlwind voice never cites laws, never cites authorities. With the Whirlwind Being creation is joy: he asks Job, "Who laid down [the earth's] cornerstone while the morning stars burst out singing and the angels shouted for joy!"

As the Whirlwind Voice spoke, what is Job experiencing? Did he hear the morning stars singing – did he actually hear the angels shouting for joy? I think he heard it and saw it both. This tight, controlling narcissistic man is suddenly encountering the divine reality. And that reality has nothing to do with rules – it is about creation.

We hear that the waters gushed from the womb of the Creator as she/he "wrapped the ocean in clouds and swaddled the sea in shadows."

Job, "Have you seen to the edge of the universe?" Job, "Where is the road to light? Where does darkness live?"

Remember Job's plan to justify the least of his actions, and to stand before God like a prince? It seems to have disappeared.

Has the Whirlwind physically caught up with Job? Is he spinning around as he encounters creation?

Job, whose wealth portfolio included thousands of domesticated animals, is now confronted with the wild ass who laughs at the driver's whip, and the wild oxen – are the wild oxen willing to serve you, Job? Fierce wild energy, but tenderness too. The Whirlwind Being eases the antelope when she is about to calve, and teaches the vulture to soar and build its nest in the clouds.

And finally we encounter the Whirlwind Being's plaything. "Look: the power in his thighs, the pulsing sinews of his belly. His penis stiffens like a pine; his testicles bulge with vigor." Hardly a domesticated animal! "You would faint at the very sight of him."

A modern equivalent might be the Crab Nebula. The Whirlwind Being might say "Look at this nebula, look at its swirling energies, its tangled vapor. Look at the spinning pulsar at its core, look at the crashing waves of energy, the orange surf bejeweled with thousands of stars." That today would be the Whirlwind's plaything.

Gone. Job's puny projection God has been swept away by divine energy. Job is free.

> I have heard of you with my ears;
> but now my eyes have seen you.
> Therefore I will be quiet,
> comforted that I am dust.

Job might have been cured of his narcissism, but has his mind been forever blown away? There is a tame after-story, stuck on the back of the Whirlwind encounter. We are told that the Lord blessed Job even more – now he had fourteen thousand sheep, and six thousand camels. And he had his children back. Well, maybe. Or maybe a scribe centuries later thought there had to be a happy ending.

But there is a bigger story. Certainly this is a story about one man's narcissism, but I think it also is a story about the narcissism of our species. For too long, humans have seen themselves as the only species that counts. Animals count for nothing. They are property, or they are there to be hunted. The Whirlwind Being totally rejects that. With savage indignation, he focuses on wild nature. Humans never appear in his cosmos.

If the after-story in the text is a scribal add-on, what is the reality? What happened to Job? I don't think he went back to wealth management. I expect Job was quiet for months, probing in his mind what had happened to him. And then I think he left Uz, and found a mountain top. I think he sat on top of the mountain listening. Listening to the sounds of nature, but also listening for the voice. Undoubtedly, he was interrupted by young Uzeans who sought advice and enlightenment from Job. But mostly, he was quiet. In spite of the terror he had felt, he yearned to hear and see and feel the Whirlwind once more.

When he was very old, he got his wish. He began to hear the voice in snatches – just bits, almost like echoes in the trees. But the voice was gentle now. It sang of small things – birds, plants and butterflies. As he traveled towards death, the voice was with him. One morning, at dawn, he suddenly heard the morning stars bursting into song, and the angels shouting for joy. Job was home.

Riddle

This is what happened. I was puzzling over the Quaker peace testimony. In particular, I wanted to know how "turn the other cheek" actually works. After all, this is a central message of Jesus's ministry (see, e.g., Mathew 5:39, 5:43; Luke 6:29–31, 6:27, 28, 32–36). It seemed to me that there was a chemistry involved, but I could not understand it. I got myself into a real knot of perplexity, with books piled up around me, and a growing frustration.

Then it suddenly occurred to me that I had just been admitted to membership in the Society of Friends (the Quakers), and I really should forget all the books and intellectual struggle and let the inner light give me the answer.

I chucked the books back on the shelf, and walked into the bathroom to get a drink of water. Bang! It happened. Right in front of me, as if a tabloid-size sheet of paper was pasted to the mirror, was a headline that read: "Tree of Life." I stared at it. Then I turned to the left. I saw through a thicket of winter branches the face of Our Lord smiling at me. His face was ablaze with light. The vision disappeared and then reappeared twice again. Needless to say, in reality, there was neither a tabloid headline, nor a thicket of branches in our bathroom.

It happened so fast, and felt so natural, that at first I did not realize that anything extraordinary had taken place. I reached for a cup and got myself some water. I went back and sat down in my study. Then I began to take in what had just happened. I felt astonishment, but I did not feel alarm, or even awe. There was an odd intimacy about the event. It baffled me, but I had the strong sense that I was supposed to be baffled. The face ablaze in the winter branches was teasing me.

It was so puzzling. How was the Tree of Life related to the peace testimony? What did Jesus's insistence that we turn the other cheek have to do with the Tree of Life?

I decided to read the mystic Julian of Norwich's *Revelation of Divine Love*. Julian had many visions, or "showings," as she called them. I realized that she had developed a methodology for probing the meaning of her visions. The visions were never dismissed as aberrant twists of the mind. She honored the vision – no matter how bizarre or even trivial they seemed, she gave her full attention to what she had experienced. She held the vision in her consciousness over a period of time, and gradually its meaning emerged. After reaching a conclusion as to its meaning, she did not dismiss the vision from her mind. She held it in her heart for the rest of her life, coming back to it again and again, and sometimes drawing a different meaning years later.

Julian's book told me that most visions are riddles, and that I must not give up on seeking to understand what I saw. This was very helpful to me.

One afternoon, Julian in the form of her wonderful book, went with me to Kew Gardens. I lay on a bench with my backpack as a pillow, read a bit of Julian, and then relaxed and ruminated about my vision. While I could not answer the riddle, I was at peace with it. I felt that eventually it would reveal its meaning.

It did. Or, it seemed to. That evening, pieces of meaning began to fall into place. And the meaning seemed as easy and natural as the vision had seemed. Here is what came to me:

First, turning the other cheek is based on treating the "evil-doer" as yourself. We move from "love your enemy" to "you are your enemy." The evil-doer you face is actually you. That's not psychological, it's organic. You and the evil-doer are united as living branches of the Tree of Life. You are the Tree of Life and so is the evil-doer. As you love your own being, so you love the evil-doer. You are embarking on a process of inviting the evil-doer into reciprocal recognition: just as you recognize the evil-doer as yourself, you are inviting the evil-doer to recognize you as him- or herself.

Watch the dynamic of power and energy. The evil-doer confronts you with power – the power to demean you, take from you, or physically harm you. This may take the form of economic or political coercion, a weapon, or simply the evil-doer's hands. The power is concentrated, tight, and trigger-ready to coerce, injure, or kill you.

Seeing the evil-doer as yourself, your response is love – you open yourself to this tense power. It is an apparent surrender to the evil-doer's power. But this apparent surrender is not passive. You are seeking to suck out – extract – the trigger-ready power which possesses the evil-doer. You are doing this by seeking to draw that power into your physical being and transform it. I'm not speaking here of the power of a weapon held by the evil-doer but the hatred, lust or cruelty that the evil-doer feels as he or she faces you. It is the force of that emotion you are seeking to encompass within yourself.

Obviously, the interface between you and the evil-doer may be moving at a speed where the hatred, lust or cruelty brings action – sometimes fatal action – almost instantly.

Perhaps I am wrong to try to work out the riddle in the context of my life as a mortal human. Perhaps the Tree of Life transcends the border between mortal life and immortal life. Maybe the meaning can only be understood in the context of one's mortal life and one's immortal life taken together. After all, Our Lord dwells simultaneously in the material world and the world beyond.

We are told in Genesis 3:22 that those who eat from the Tree of Life gain immortality. God hastened Adam and Eve out of Eden for fear that they would eat the fruit of the Tree of Life and become immortal. God stationed the cherubim and the fiery ever-turning sword to guard the way to the Tree of Life (Genesis 3:24). Was Jesus promising the fruit of the Tree of Life to those that turn the other cheek? Is he inviting into immortal life those that follow his teaching on not resisting evil?

What does that mean? Is it an acknowledgment that if you follow Jesus's mandate you are apt to lose your natural life? Or is the "immortal life" offered by the Tree of Life something that transcends the dichotomy between mortal and immortal life? Is it a life – and indeed a mortal life – which is infused with the reality of immortality? Where the human living his mortal life can experience with his or her senses the full delights of the Creator's work?

Jesus alluded to mortals who are walking dead. "Let the dead bury the dead," he told a would-be follower who pleaded the necessity of first burying his father (Mathew 8:22, Luke 9:60). These mortally living dead close themselves off from the fruits of the Tree of Life – they dare not embark on adventures that involve actual creation. Perhaps the most deadening thing you can do is to give evil for evil – and in contrast, perhaps turning the other cheek – the daring of it, the adventure of it – will open you to direct experience of the Creator.

Symbiosis

I am fascinated by the potentiality of human consciousness.

The Creator made humans in his or her own image. That does not mean that the Creator has toenails like us. It means that we have consciousness like the Creator. We were gifted a consciousness potentially as deep and broad as the Creator's own consciousness. That's what defines us as a species.

Self-awareness may be all but universal in the natural world. And in some animals sentience is well developed. But human consciousness surely is unique. I think we can expand our consciousness almost infinitely. Now empathetic individuals can feel what another human is feeling – what the individual is going through. And if we have a dog, we can feel what that companionable beast is feeling.

Is it too hard to imagine that pioneers might one day be able to feel what a tree is feeling? Might that capacity of perception become part of human culture, to be built upon generation by generation?

Perhaps one day we humans uniquely will have what I might call a *unitary consciousness* – a consciousness so sensitive that as we pass through an environment, we can experience what all living beings around us are feeling.

The development of a unitary consciousness between humans and the natural world would open the door to astonishing sensations. Imagine: you are sitting below a flowering laburnum. You hear the low buzz of bumblebees.

And you momentarily feel what the laburnum feels. Its blossoms are the most sensitive part of its physical being. The blossoms have opened themselves. The bumblebee buzzes with excitement and lands on the lower petal of the blossom. It pushes its way into the flower, sensing the nectar that will be its reward. And the tree feels that penetration, feels the vibrations of the buzzing bee. The tree feels repleteness as the bee penetrates, and it senses the delicate dusting of the bee's buzzing body as it is covered with its pollen. The laburnum feels this simultaneously in hundreds of blossoms being serviced by hundreds of bees. The Creator can feel the tree's ecstasy. Potentially, you can too. That is the promise of the Creator's gift of consciousness.

Human consciousness could play a role in physical reality that is inconceivable to us now. As consciousness evolves and we share in the sensations of the natural world, a new energy will arise. An energy of delight. Our souls will thrive in that energy. But the promise of unitary consciousness is that the tree will share in the new human consciousness. It will share in that energy of delight. The tree will thrive as never before.

Buddha and the Bo Tree

Siddhartha, the future Buddha, sat under the Bo tree (*Ficus religiosa*; also known as the bodhi tree or peepul tree) around 500 BCE. He remained there for forty-nine days before obtaining enlightenment. I can't find a Buddhist text that tells us what Siddhartha felt from the Bo tree – whether he believed the Bo tree helped him reach enlightenment or not. But he honored the tree, and later instructed his disciple Ananda to plant Bo trees elsewhere. I am very curious about what happened between the Buddha and the Bo tree. In the absence of any information about what Siddhartha felt from the Bo tree, I have speculated about what the Bo tree experienced while Siddhartha sat beneath it.

To do that, I needed to explore the nature of the Bo tree's experience of life. The Bo tree was home to hundreds of life-forms: insects, lizards, snakes, small mammals, and myriad birds. I think there was a unity of consciousness between the Bo tree and these living beings. I believe they shared a unitary consciousness. That consciousness was complex – each creature felt the world in its own unique way but without effort participated in the consciousness of everything else.

At the apex of this unitary consciousness was the king cobra, Nagaraja, who lived in the earth, in a cavern formed by the Bo tree's roots. In this dark cavern, the snake coiled amongst the tree's roots, and felt each pulse of the tree's life. And the tree felt awareness of the snake, and delighted in its smooth slithering travel across its limbs, delighted in the whispered sensations Nagaraja picked up with his ever-active forked tongue.

We know now that the ends of tree roots have intelligence – some say that the brain of the tree is in the ends of the roots. The roots are dynamic. Their ends explore, looking for nutrients to nourish the tree and the tree's community. Mycorrhizal fungi, those thin filaments you see in the soil, extend the roots, forming an intimate network with plants and beings. Trees have a rich awareness of their environment through their roots and through the mycorrhizal fungi. Through the root and fungal network, the tree can also export nutrients to young or needy organisms.

Into this community of sensation and connection came Siddhartha. He circled the tree several times, and then sat down cross-legged facing east. Silence. The chatter of all the tree-beings is stilled. The tree's heart-shaped leaves measure the shadow cast by this slight figure. Every sense of this complex organic consciousness is focused on Siddhartha. They watch, they smell. They listen to Siddhartha's breathing. They want to feel his physical being. This was the first time this community of consciousness was focused on one particular being.

The Bo tree itself is beguiled by the gentle being, and feels a needfulness it has never felt with any other human. Siddhartha has been sitting five days, and has taken in no food or drink. The watching and listening organisms, and the tree itself, yearn to nurture Siddhartha. Such is the habitual response of the tree to organisms in need. The roots near

Siddhartha fill with sun-created nutrients. The roots come close to the flesh of Siddhartha as he sits on the ground cross-legged. The roots want to touch, want to explore, want to succor this being. And the tree organisms want Siddhartha to be one with the tree's family of beings.

So, over days, a delicate growth of new twigs caress and shelter the golden body. The Bo tree's roots explore the contour of Siddhartha's flesh. Tiny roots find a way to tenderly grow into him. Siddhartha's body accepts the nutrients the roots bring. The body of the Siddhartha sends back in loving symbiosis a peace and a vitality never before felt by the tree – an energy immediately shared with all in the tree's family of organisms. And now in soft companionability a red-whiskered bulbul bird perches on one shoulder, and a jungle babbler rests on the other. A gecko sits contentedly on Siddhartha's thigh.

Nagaraja is near Siddhartha. He lies on the tree limbs above. He flicks his tongue. Day by day, the cobra is there, and it is Nagaraja who senses something growing, a new light within Siddhartha, at first barely perceptible but now growing stronger and burgeoning – an energy never before encountered. The cobra drops from his branch and moves across the still body. He wraps himself around Siddhartha. He feels Siddhartha drawing out of him earth wisdom, and he feels Siddhartha's light coming into him. All that Nagaraja feels the tree feels and all the myriad beings in the tree feel. The light within Siddhartha saturates the tree and its community, and now that light begins to saturate the world.

The black drongo bird senses the danger first. The Powers that control humans and exploit the natural world have awakened to the golden energy being released by Siddhartha's body. They react with panic. What will this golden energy do to their control? They sense subversion. This could be a revolution! The Powers are deathly afraid. Their reaction: destroy Siddhartha! They conjure a great storm focused directly on the Bo tree, directly on Siddhartha.

The tree feels it coming. Ever-alert Nagaraja manifests his ancient chthonic shape and rears above Siddhartha, now seven-headed. He spreads his hoods making a shelter for the golden one, weaving back and forth to meet the fierce power of the storm. Siddhartha never moves, but his energy begins to saturate the storm, and the storm moderates, slows, turns into a soft rain, and then into a mist which enwraps the tree. The Powers rage, but they are baffled.

Nine days later Lord Buddha achieves enlightenment. But he does not yet arise and go forth to enlighten the world. He pauses, and remains for a week under the Bo tree, one with the tree and each of the insects, lizards, snakes, small mammals, and myriad birds that live in the tree. The Bo tree and all its family of organisms become sacred.

Dreaming Verses

To me, some stories about Jesus and his disciples are best understood as dream sequences. Here is one, a piece of Verse 21 in the Gospel of Thomas:

> Mary asked Jesus, "Whom are your disciples like?"

> He said, "they are like children who have settled in a field which is not theirs. When the owners of the field come, they will say, 'Let us have back our field.' They will undress in their presence in order to let them have back their field and to give it back to them."

I could not make sense of this until I let it rest in my mind as a dream, visually. Dreams are full of unexpected events and non sequiturs. They often baffle our rational minds, but tell us truths on another level. So I opened myself to a dream reading of the verse.

Envision this: the disciples are exhausted. They have left the country around the Sea of Galilee. Jesus has talked to them, told them that he will be rejected by the elders, the chief priests, and the doctors of the law. He has told them that he will be turned over to the Romans and crucified, and that after three days he will rise again from the dead.

The disciples are dumbfounded. They cannot take it in. They are horrified. Peter is so shaken that he takes Jesus aside and rebukes him for saying such a thing. Jesus is very angry with Peter.

Now they are climbing into the hills to the north, on the road to Caesarea Philippi. The air is becoming cooler. But the disciples do not notice. They are numb, some angry, all baffled.

Jesus stops them on the road just over halfway up. He turns and points.

"Look!" he says.

They turn, and there spread before them is the Sea of Galilee with Mount Tabor off in the distance. They stand and look. Jesus points out Capernaum, Gennesaret, Magdala and Tiberias. The disciples are captivated by what their eyes see.

Jesus does not hurry them. He stands back and watches each one, and sees the distress begin to lift from their shoulders. He watches as they sigh and wipe their faces. They share water from a skin.

"Come. She is waiting for us."

They drink in the view one more time, and turn, following Jesus. He leads them higher. The road moves to the right around a rocky outcrop. They push on. Cedars now shade their way. The air is sweet. When the road levels out, Jesus leads them off to the left on a path running through the cedars. Then, around a bend, they see it: a great sweep of color. It is a field of flowers: narcissus, pink flax, iris, borage, and wild anemones.

They stand spellbound.

Then Jesus sings out, "Jerusalem, take off your dress of sorrows and distress."

The disciples immediately respond, "Put on the beauty of the Creator's glory for evermore."

Singing back and forth, the disciples and Jesus slowly enter the field. Their faces are open now, their eyes soft. The disciples are becoming like children.

Jesus sings again, "Jerusalem, take off your dress of sorrows and distress."

The disciples respond, "Put the diadem of the Eternal One's glory upon your head."

They tiptoe among the flowers until they reach a huge cedar tree. The water of a spring emerges from among its roots forming a pool on one side surrounded by soft grass. They settle here, taking their ease. Peter is already lying under the tree, looking up through the branches. Jesus sits beside him. Into Peter's mind come words of Ezekiel:

A cedar tree in Lebanon,
A cedar tree with noble branches, dense foliage,
Lofty height. Its top pierces the clouds.
In its boughs all the birds of the air have their nests.
Under its branches all wild creatures bear their young.
And in its shadows all great nations make their home.
There is no tree like it in the garden of God.

They sleep under the tree, and then spend three days resting. They are silent for the most part, watching the beauty of the flowers and the nobility of the ancient cedar. Occasionally, they sing back and forth among themselves.

At peace, their surroundings begin to clothe them. At first it is barely noticeable. But then it happens. John's clothes are first. His worn robe begins to glow with the color of the anemones. Soon the colors of the iris and the narcissus emerge, and then the form and even the scent of the flowers.

It happens to each one of them, but each is different. Judas's cloak is the pink of the pink flax. Levi's is the deep blue of the iris, shot through with gold and lines of jet. Peter's is the yellow of the narcissus. They are attired like the lilies of the field, each in splendor. After the gift of its flowers, the field is left a soft green meadow.

Now we see the arrival of the owners. Serious, practical men. Three of them. The men are angry with the trespassers. "Let us have our field back!"

The disciples stare at them. They hesitate, but after a moment they begin to undress. They take off their gossamer garments and hand them to the owners. The owners are shocked and indignant.

"Stop! What are you doing? Don't give us these filthy rags!"

The owners throw the clothes on the ground. The clothes lie on the soft green grass of the field. Then, in an instant, the flowers pour off them, flowing back onto the field until the field again is covered with blooms.

The disciples stand naked. They smile at the owners.

"Do not pollute our eyes with your shameful nakedness! Take your rags! Go!"

Slowly each disciple picks up his own clothes, now very ordinary, patched and well-worn, and puts them on. Jesus comes out of the field, and they follow him as he walks towards the road.

They walk up the road silently. Then Jesus glances at James, and suddenly they are all laughing. They laugh for sheer joy. They laugh so hard they can barely stand up.

Above them, puffy white clouds parade across an azure sky. Crickets sing, and swallows swoop and twitter.

Behold the Lamb of God

John the Baptist pointed at Jesus as he walked by. "Behold the Lamb of God," he said. Two of his disciples heard John the Baptist say this and followed Jesus.

The two that followed Jesus were abashed when Jesus turned and asked:

"What do you seek?"

Their lame response was "Where are you staying?"

"Come and see," was the reply.

They followed Jesus, watching him with curiosity. They were hungry souls, searching, hoping.

Andrew was one of the two disciples. Was the other John? I think so. When Jesus reached the dwelling where he was staying, he invited them in. They sat down. Jesus asked them about their lives. He probably looked at them with gentle searching eyes. Andrew, the older of the two, talked the most. John watched. John was much younger than Andrew, and Andrew had a way of talking over him. Andrew, nervous and uneasy, undoubtedly went on for too long. He may have shown Jesus the scar he had from cutting his leg when he fell out of his boat. Jesus touched Andrew's scar, and Andrew was surprised that the tightness of the scar was eased. Andrew had never been listened to so intently, and he began to tell Jesus about deeply personal memories. Jesus listened. Then with sure insight Jesus suggested to Andrew what these events meant to him. What Jesus said seemed to liberate Andrew. To his great embarrassment, he began to cry. Jesus reached over and touched his hand. "It's alright, Andrew."

Jesus began to teach them. He explained the real meaning of scripture, telling them things they'd never heard before.

"Now that I am with you, with you Andrew, and you John, and I will tell you what has been secret." Jesus paused. Then he said, "The law, the law of Moses, with all of its hundreds of rules, comes down to just two things." Jesus again paused.

"What are they?" asked John hesitantly.

"Shh," said Andrew.

"They are this, John. Love your neighbor as yourself, and love God. And, Andrew, these two rules are the same."

Andrew's mouth fell open. He rubbed his head. He was thinking of the laws on the preparation of food that his family carefully followed. Finally he said, "But Rabbi, how can that be? What about the prohibition against eating pork? What about the rule on unclean women?"

"And what about the law prohibiting work on the Sabbath?" Jesus asked. "I will break that law. I will cure the sick on the Sabbath. Why? Because in his love for each of us, God feels our pain. He yearns to cure us of our sicknesses. Our needs are his needs. I am God's love. So when I feel a person's pain, I will cure it, even if it happens to be the Sabbath."

He taught them gently, but as he led them, his visage glowed, and the two felt wonder. His words made their souls replete. They felt a deep content in their bodies they had never felt before. Andrew sighed. "I must go and find my brother Simon Peter, and bring him to you, Master."

John was left alone with Jesus.

All his life John had felt the vital beings of plants and trees, and even rocks. They seemed to talk to him. He wanted to tell Jesus about this. He was sure that Jesus had the same energy that he had felt in the natural world – but even more so. He started to tell Jesus, but he found he was incoherent – he couldn't say what he meant. Jesus reached out and took John's hand.

"Yes, John, I am all of that, and so are you." John barely heard that because he was amazed by what he felt when Jesus held his hand – a sweet compelling energy. It was wonderful, but frightening too. He pulled his hand away. After a moment John dared to look at Jesus. Jesus smiled at him. John suddenly smiled too. He was completely happy. John reached out his hand, and Jesus took it.

Meanwhile, Andrew had found his brother Simon Peter. "Simon! We have found the Messiah!"

Beloved Disciple

Can a disciple be an enabler? Can a devoted disciple draw out from the teacher what otherwise might not be taught?

When Jesus taught, one of his disciples watched and listened, utterly absorbed. That was John, the beloved disciple. The other disciples listened, and gave attention to Jesus, but they were often wrestling with their mental habits, which meant they were often baffled by what Jesus said. Not John. He could follow the flow of Jesus's speech. To John each word was a glistening gift. Each word was an invitation to enter another world – the Kingdom that Jesus promised. Jesus's words caressed John's soul. They opened him, and John surrendered to them with a spiritual ecstasy.

Perhaps this was in part the result of John's youth. Perhaps it was a result of Jesus's protective tenderness towards him.

Jesus felt John's openness, and felt John's passion for absorbing his teaching. When Jesus spoke, he looked into the eyes of first one disciple and then another. What he often saw was puzzlement and a struggle to understand. Sometimes he saw hostility. Often his words were shocking, even painful to many of his disciples. But when Jesus looked into John's eyes, he saw John's ecstasy and excitement. And he saw John's love.

It must have been exciting to Jesus to feed John's spiritual hunger. Perhaps there were times when Jesus's words were addressed primarily to John. And perhaps John's love drew out of Jesus spiritual teachings that were too mystical for the other disciples to understand. Perhaps Jesus had insights, and thought thoughts, he would not have had without John's beguiling spiritual hunger always seeking more.

Those teachings, enabled by John's love, is what makes John's Gospel so different from the other three.

Easter

The Easter story: observe how simple it is. There is no chorus of angels. No thunder. No whirlwind. It is calm – and, in an odd way, ordinary.

Let's work backward from Jesus's encounter with Mary Magdalene. There comes a time when Jesus got up off that stone ledge where they had laid his body in the tomb. He sits for a moment, and then begins to unwind the grave clothes. He pauses, and takes in the sensation of being alive. He looks at his hands. The terrible wounds are all but healed. He looks at the wound in his side. It too is healing. He is aware of his breathing – breathing! He smiles. He stretches. He is alive.

Yes, in that dark night of the soul, dead, in hell – but no, that's not the way it was. He found her, the eternal female. He and she came together, they became one, and now he is her and she is him. He is whole. And he is content now, at peace, and oh, so excited to see his followers. He stands up, picks up the grave clothes and folds them neatly. There is something funny about this. His mother always insisted that he fold his night clothes and put them under his pillow.

He walks. It feels good. Now, here is the rock at the entrance of the tomb. He thinks of Jacob moving the stone that sat atop Lamach's well. He thinks, "I'll move the stone, open the grave, and drink in life on the other side." He gives the stone a push. Um. Stubborn. So he gives it a stronger push – and it rolls. He is free!

The world floods into him. The tenderness of it all! So soft. He is enrapt in the fresh scent of waking nature. The stars are fading in the coming light. He stands. Breathes. He can see around him an old garden. A neglected garden. Plants push up in response to the warm air of spring, but they look stunted. Look how compacted the earth is. And here are fresh footprints around the plants, sometimes on top of them. People must have accompanied his dead body to this tomb.

"Ah," he thinks to himself, "here is a hoe – and this must be the gardener's work tunic. Well, I'll put that on. People might be shocked by my nakedness." He picks up the hoe – its oak handle feels good in his hands. "I will open up the earth," he says to himself, "I will make it porous to the air." The earth first, and then humans. So, he works the garden, breaking up the hard ground, propping up the plants that were stepped on. And he knows that his new being is seeding the earth, that it will grow and blossom. "I will seed each person and grow and blossom within them. I will be their light."

The sun will soon be up. A chorus of birds celebrate. And now he senses an arrival. Mary! Oh, Mary! Beautiful Mary! She hastens over to the entrance to the tomb. She looks in. He hears her gasp. Now she looks at the stone that he pushed aside.

"Where is he? They have stolen the body of my beloved!"

She turns and sees him. She doesn't recognize him. "Sir, if you have taken him away, tell me where you put him."

"Mary."

The light is coming up. She stands stock-still. She stares at him. She turns and looks back at the empty tomb. She is trembling now.

"Rabbani?" she whispers.

"Yes, Mary, it's me."

She rushes to him, falls on her knees and embraces his legs.

He leans over and holds her. "Mary, Mary, don't be afraid. It's me. I've come back."

He lifts her up and embraces her.

"Oh, oh, I can't understand. Oh, sweet Lord, you were dead. They were so cruel. Look, your wounds. They have healed. How?" She pulls away from him. "Oh, Rabbani, you are different! I touch you, and you are warm, but..."

She falls on her knees again. "So it is true, all that you said."

"Yes, it is true. I've come back, and now I will dwell in the human heart. Never again will I judge humanity."

She is crying now, looking up at him through her tears. Jesus smiles at her. "Mary, you must go tell the others. Tell them I will meet them in Galilee."

Mary covers her eyes, overcome. When she looks again, he is gone. She slowly gets up. She stands, immobile. Was that real? Was she dreaming? She looks back at the empty tomb, and then she knows. She runs to tell the others.

Peace of the Lord

I went to the secret place, and as I went I began to see sacred things. Complex actualities of lichen-covered branches, ragged flowers, cotoneaster splaying across the overgrown path. I paused by the sea buckthorns, and stared through its branches to the pond. I went further to the abandoned bench, and rested there for a while. Then I went and rubbed myself against the fissured bark of the ancient alder. I listened to the breeze. I watched the tangle of dark roots in the water, and the sun in quiet play on the smooth branches. The alder sang to me. I sank into meditation.

When I emerged, a female mallard duck was on the pond's wall in front of me. She had a jolting vitality in her feather patterns that I had never seen before. She watched her two-week old ducklings zigzag across the pond. Then she gathered them up on the bank in the leafy shadow of the large branch. The little ones huddled into a fuzzy little pod and went to sleep, and the mum slept too.

The limb of the alder bent over them protectively, as if that was what it was for. The relationship of duck and tree was whole and ancient, and unlike the jittery attempt at a relationship that I have worked to achieve.

I watched, and knew that what I felt was the peace of the Lord that surpasses all understanding.

The Presence

I am in love. But the being I love escapes, then returns, then
teases, then thrills. What is this being? Is it a him or a her? I
do not know. Yet I feel so often after an event, or an
encounter, that the event or encounter included somebody
wonderful – somebody who is just the friend or companion
or lover I need. Afterwards I wonder, *what made that so
special*? What made it feel so spacious, so generous? I think
of who was there or who I saw, and then I realize that, yes,
the people I saw were wonderful, but it was someone else
who deepened my relationship with them, and that someone
was him or her, this ever-playful, ever-loving being.

This being is just out of range, just beyond what I can see,
but definitely there. Yes, I love this being with all my heart.
If I could meet him or her face-to-face, what would I do?
Dance. Maybe dance. Caper. Be a fool. Tease him about his
elusiveness, about her peeking into my world, but definitely I
would tell her how much I love her.

This being is certainly not magisterial or portentous. Nor
is this being a mere sprite. Within the galaxy of my being,
he/she is like a flower. How happy I would be to merge with
her, be the wine of her life, because he is more perfectly me
than I am.

Endnotes

Called to Silence

Evelyn Underhill, *The Cloud of Unknowing* (Element Classics of World Spirituality, 1997). She rendered the original text into modern English. John Main (1926–82) was a priest in the Order of St. Benedict whose lifework led to the foundation of the World Community for Christian Meditation. He sought to bring into modern Christian worship the tradition of meditative prayer originated by the Desert Fathers in the 4th century.

Numbed

Gary Snyder (1930–) is an American poet, teacher, hiker, essayist, and one-time Zen monk. In 1974 he published *Turtle Island* (New Directions, 1974), which won the Pulitzer Prize for Poetry. The best way to meet him is to watch the film *The Practice of the Wild*, directed by John J. Healey, Whole Earth Films, 2010. The trailer is on YouTube. The quote is from Snyder's poem "By Frazer Creek Falls" in *Turtle Island*.

Rainer Maria Rilke (1875–1926) was an Austrian poet and novelist. He wrote the *Duino Elegies, Sonnets to Orpheus,* and *Letters to a Young Poet.* Search YouTube for the TV documentary *Rainer Maria Rilke: Letters to a Young Poet,* directed by Stan Neumann in 1996. The quote is from the "Eighth Elegy" in the *Duino Elegies*.

Saint Antony of the Desert (251–356) as a young man sold all his worldly goods and gave the proceeds to the poor. Thereafter, he lived in complete solitude for fourteen years in the ruins of a Roman fort in the desert. Here he underwent the temptations depicted by Hieronymus Bosch and others. Later, he left his solitude in order to teach his many disciples. Together they are are known as the Desert Fathers – although they included women. Famously, he went in search of the first hermit, Paul. With the help of a satyr, Antony found Paul, and they both were fed by a raven who dropped bread to them. Athanasius of Alexandria wrote a biography of Antony between 356 and 362, *Life of Antony*.

The Douglas E. Christie quote is from *The Blue Sapphire of the Mind: Notes for a Contemplative Ecology* (Oxford University Press 2012, page 81). Douglas E. Christie is a professor of theology at Loyola Marymount University in Los Angeles. He holds graduate degrees from Oxford and the Graduate Theological Union, Berkley. He is also the author of *The Word in the Desert: Scripture and the Quest for Early Christian Monasticism* (Oxford University Press 1993) and *The Insurmountable Darkness of Love: Mysticism, Loss and the Common Life* (Oxford University Press 2022). He is the founding editor of the journal

Spiritus (John Hopkins University Press). You can find out more about his work by watching the interview *Spiritual Perception and the Natural World with Douglas Christie* on YouTube.

Resist Power, Be Energy

The artist Michelangelo di Lodovico Buonarroti Simoni, known as Michelangelo, created the sculpture of David from 1501 to 1504. The original is in the Accademia Galleria in Florence, Italy. Some of the best pictures are of the cast in the Victoria and Albert Museum in London. See collections.vam.ac.uk/item/O39861/david-statue-michelangelo.

The Guanyin Bodhisattva sculpture, made around 1200, is at the Victoria and Albert Museum. If you enter Guanyin Bodhisattva "V&A A-7-1935" on the V&A website you can view its picture. Here is the URL: collections.vam.ac.uk/item/O72412/guanyin-figure-of-gua nyin-unknown.

Andrei Rublev is thought to have been born sometime around the 1360s and died in the Andronikov Monastery in Moscow between 1427 and 1430. He was a monk and icon painter. His *Trinity* is thought to have been painted in the early 15th century. The director Andrei Tarkovsky made a film, *Andrei Rublev*, (Mosfilm, 1966) based loosely on the artist's life. It is available to watch on YouTube.

Soft Eyes

Rembrandt was born in 1606 and died in 1669. He painted 27 self-portraits. They are reflective, moving and deeply honest to my eye. *Portrait of the Artist as a Young Man* may be viewed online here: liverpoolmuseums.org.uk/artifact/portrait-of-artist-young-man.

Meditation on Saxifrage

Vasily Semyonovich Grossman was born in 1905 and died in 1964. He was a writer and journalist. Grossman finished *Life and Fate* in 1959, but it was not published in the Soviet Union until 1980. After he wrote the book, the KGB raided his apartment and confiscated his manuscript and notes. Robert Chandler, his translator, gave a lecture called *Vasily Grossman, heroic witness and supreme artist* which is available on YouTube.

Should She Be Stoned?

The painting *Woman Taken in Adultery* is by Giovanni Francesco Barbieri (1591–1666); he is known as Guercino or "squint-eyed." It was painted about 1621. You can view it on the Dulwich Picture Gallery website here: dulwichpicturegallery.org.uk/explore-the-collection/251-300/the-woman-taken-in-adultery.

The Silent Music of Psalm 19

In Dante's *Purgatorio*, Virgil, Dante's guide and mentor, says:

"The heavens call to you, and wheel about you, revealing their eternal splendors, but your eyes are fixed upon the earth..."

Purgatorio, Canto XIV, lines 148–151 (Hollander translation).

Dreaming Verses

The Gospel of Thomas was one of the texts found at Nag Hammadi in Egypt in 1945. It is often characterized as a gnostic gospel.

The quote is from Ezekiel 31.

Job Revisited

My efforts to discern the meaning of the Book of Job were greatly helped by William Blake's *Illustrations of the Book of Job*, and by Stephen Mitchell's wonderful translation (Stephen Mitchell, *The Book of Job*, Harper Perennial, 1992). The quotes are all from Mitchell's translation except the one beginning "Don't poach..." I made that one up.

The Blake illustrations were first published by Blake in 1826 as *Illustrations of the Book of Job in Twenty-One Plates, Invented and Engraved by William Blake*. A modern edition was published in 2015.

Job's Evil Dreams (Plate 11) is available online here: hrc.contentdm.oclc.org/digital/collection/p15878coll93/id/ 59.

Riddle

Julian of Norwich, 1342 to about 1416, was an anchoress living as a shut-in in a hermitage next to a parish church in Norwich. At thirty-one years old she suffered a nearly fatal illness, and during that illness she had a series of sixteen visions or "showings." About fifteen years later she had one more showing that confirmed that all that she had seen and experienced was God's love. She tells us that God lives in our souls, and thirsts and longs for us. And she tells us that Christ is our mother. She is optimistic. She tells us that "all will be well, and every kind of thing will be well."

She wrote two books: the so-called *Short Text*, written soon after the visions, and many years later, the *Long Text*, which reflect her consideration of the visions after many years. These books are the first books written by a woman in English – as far as we know. See Julian of Norwich, *Revelations of Divine Love*.

The differences between the *Short Text* and the *Long Text* reflect her many years of discernment as to the deeper meaning of her visions. This is particularly evident in chapter 51 of the *Long Text* where meaning emerges in the Parable of the Lord and his Servant.

Acknowledgments

My editor, Tanya Williams, brought this project to fruition. Without her, this material would have sat on my computer indefinitely. Many thanks to her. The Richmond Meeting of the Society of Friends suffered through "ministries" where I sought to articulate what became these little pieces. Thanks to them for their patience. The Rt. Rev. Eugene Sutton, now Episcopal Bishop of Maryland, greatly helped me as I began my exploration of contemplative prayer. Howard Means was always generous in his encouragement, and had the fortitude to read two of my earlier manuscripts. Isabella Bates was my spiritual mentor for many years, and carefully reviewed this manuscript. The Royal Botanic Gardens, Kew, exists on the threshold between this world and the divine world, and time meditating there was pivotal to the insights I set out here. My wife Mary has helped me find the time to write, and she has, each year, given me the gift of membership in the London Library. Many, many thanks to her. My children, Mark, Derek and Eleanor have amused me marvelously; wonderful breaks from the sometimes trying work of writing, and my grandchildren have joyfully joined in their efforts. Derek worked on the final transcript and his expertise in publishing has been a much appreciated reality check for me. His friend Jaakko designed the beautiful cover. Many thanks to him. Many others have helped me in numerous ways – to all, my heartfelt thanks.

Ben Lamberton is 83. He lives in London with his wife. His three children and six grandchildren also live in London. He is a volunteer litter-picker in Kew Gardens.

Printed in Poland
by Amazon Fulfillment
Poland Sp. z o.o., Wrocław
30 November 2023

7b024167-374b-4d62-91cd-1b3337178438R02